WOMEN OVER
30
ARE BETTER BECAUSE

Written By:
Herbert Kavet

Illustrated By:
Martin Riskin

30 29 28 27 26 25 24 23 22 21 20 19 18 17 16 15 14 13 12 11 10 9 8 7 6 5 4 3 2 1

Ivory Tower Publishing Co., Inc.
125 Walnut St., Watertown, MA 02172
Telephone #: (617) 923-1111   Fax #: (617) 923-8839

WOMEN OVER **30** ARE BETTER BECAUSE...

They get lots more respect from the banking community.

WOMEN OVER **30** ARE BETTER BECAUSE...

They check to see if their blind dates have cars.

WOMEN OVER 30 ARE BETTER BECAUSE...

People start to admire their mind as much as their body.

WOMEN OVER **30** ARE BETTER BECAUSE...

They prefer sex to be enchanting rather than athletic.

WOMEN OVER 30 ARE BETTER BECAUSE...

They finally recognize the value of control top pantyhose.

WOMEN OVER **30** ARE BETTER BECAUSE...

Their personality doesn't change when a man is around.

WOMEN OVER **30** ARE BETTER BECAUSE...

They know how to keep a secret.

WOMEN OVER 30 ARE BETTER BECAUSE...

They know nothing is more comfortable than an old running shoe.

WOMEN OVER **30** ARE BETTER BECAUSE...

They are resigned to the fact that they will never use their college education to earn a living.

WOMEN OVER **30** ARE BETTER BECAUSE...

They can handle it when all their friends get engaged.

WOMEN OVER 30 ARE BETTER BECAUSE...

They don't mind one bit
going to a movie alone on a Saturday night.

WOMEN OVER **30** ARE BETTER BECAUSE...

They no longer let the men in their life talk them into fishing and camping trips.

WOMEN OVER 30 ARE BETTER BECAUSE...

They've learned the dangers of being a matchmaker.

They are not easily intimidated in traffic.

WOMEN OVER **30** ARE BETTER BECAUSE...

Their handbags can sustain life for about a week with no outside support whatsoever.

WOMEN OVER **30** ARE BETTER BECAUSE...

They're finally treated with more respect at work.

They have a handle on the latest fashions.

WOMEN OVER **30** ARE BETTER BECAUSE...

They've learned how to dress to suit their figure.

WOMEN OVER **30** ARE BETTER BECAUSE...

They don't go on blind dates.

WOMEN OVER **30** ARE BETTER BECAUSE...

They have become bewilderingly efficient in their jobs.

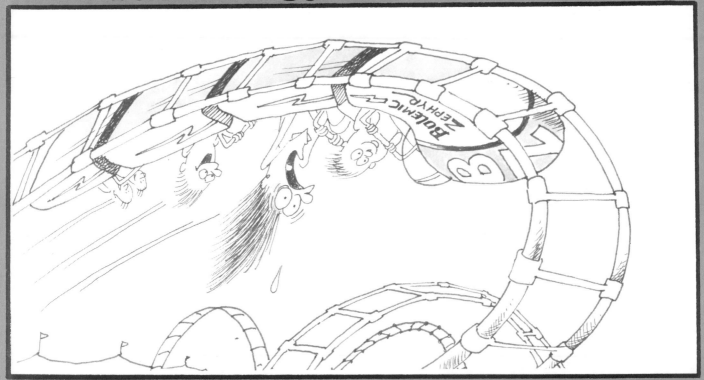

They can't be talked into activities they don't like.

WOMEN OVER **30** ARE BETTER BECAUSE...

They've learned not to recommend hairdressers.

WOMEN OVER 30 ARE BETTER BECAUSE...

They occasionally clean their ovens.

WOMEN OVER **30** ARE BETTER BECAUSE...

They occasionally defrost their freezers.

They can afford to take some really exotic vacations.

WOMEN OVER 30 ARE BETTER BECAUSE...

They know just what it takes to make a man feel good.

They receive offers for credit cards on a regular basis.

WOMEN OVER **30** ARE BETTER BECAUSE...

They no longer have trouble getting into bars.

WOMEN OVER **30** ARE BETTER BECAUSE...

They've developed some decorating schemes of their own.

WOMEN OVER **30** ARE BETTER BECAUSE...

They don't freak out when their mother comes to stay for a few days.

WOMEN OVER **30** ARE BETTER BECAUSE...

They no longer run out of underwear.

They're not embarrassed to use a little ingenuity in the bedroom.

WOMEN OVER **30** ARE BETTER BECAUSE...

They understand about "closing costs."

They can buy a new car without their father's advice.

They've learned how to say "NO" to men bugging them for dates.

They can afford an occasional splurge.

WOMEN OVER **30** ARE BETTER BECAUSE...

They can program the VCR for their fathers.

WOMEN OVER 30 ARE BETTER BECAUSE...

They've started to understand the male psyche a little better.

WOMEN OVER **30** ARE BETTER BECAUSE...

They've reached a sort of accommodation with their pets.

WOMEN OVER **30** ARE BETTER BECAUSE...

They remember the abrasive qualities of sand
before making love on a beach.

They can fit almost all their makeup into a carry-on.

They're not afraid to
complain about poor workmanship on their car.

WOMEN OVER **30** ARE BETTER BECAUSE...

They're smart enough to handle certain chores on a regular basis.

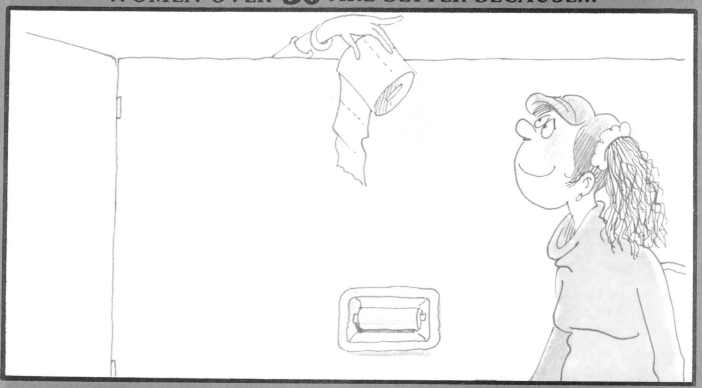

They truly know the value of a good friend.

WOMEN OVER 30 ARE BETTER BECAUSE...

97% of all their sex takes place in a bed.

WOMEN OVER **30** ARE BETTER BECAUSE...

They're not bashful about asking people not to smoke.

*They can eat a double hot fudge sundae
and probably not "break out."*

WOMEN OVER **30** ARE BETTER BECAUSE...

They are beginning to fantasize about going into business for themselves.

WOMEN OVER 30 ARE BETTER BECAUSE...

They realize none of the courses they took in college have the slightest value to them now.

WOMEN OVER **30** ARE BETTER BECAUSE...

They know how to organize a truly great party.

WOMEN OVER **30** ARE BETTER BECAUSE...

They read the reviews before they go to a show.

WOMEN OVER **30** ARE BETTER BECAUSE...

They appreciate the warmth and comfort of flannel nighties.

They know all the tricks for starting a car on a really cold day.

WOMEN OVER **30** ARE BETTER BECAUSE...

They've started to choose vacations for peace and quiet rather than action.

WOMEN OVER **30** ARE BETTER BECAUSE...

They know a few off-color stories of their own.

They don't get embarrassed introducing their friends to weird relatives.

WOMEN OVER 30 ARE BETTER BECAUSE...

They've stopped waiting for the baby fat to disappear.

WOMEN OVER 30 ARE BETTER BECAUSE...

The phone and electric companies hardly ever disconnect their service.

WOMEN OVER **30** ARE BETTER BECAUSE...

*They recognize that
sex in the water is at best uncomfortable and
at worst potentially life threatening.*

WOMEN OVER **30** ARE BETTER BECAUSE...

They still look pretty good in a bathing suit.

WOMEN OVER **30** ARE BETTER BECAUSE...

They're intimately familiar with every diet that came along in the last 10 years.

WOMEN OVER **30** ARE BETTER BECAUSE...

They've developed total confidence in "woman's intuition."

They diet when brushing their teeth causes them to jiggle.

WOMEN OVER **30** ARE BETTER BECAUSE...

Most of their wines have corks rather than screw tops.

They can handle an occasional kinky request.

WOMEN OVER **30** ARE BETTER BECAUSE...

They are starting to acquire some matching furnishings.

WOMEN OVER **30** ARE BETTER BECAUSE...

They make plans to wash their kitchen floor.

They have an outstanding collection of bridesmaid dresses.

They know it's impossible to change people's habits.

They'd rather have their men successful than good-looking.

They have a few secret recipes for emergency dinners.

WOMEN OVER **30** ARE BETTER BECAUSE...

They know how to use 4 letter words at appropriate moments.

WOMEN OVER 30 ARE BETTER BECAUSE...

They don't blush at X-rated movies.

They finally own a car that is totally paid for.

They have learned to use restraint at big sales.

WOMEN OVER 30 ARE BETTER BECAUSE...

They can remember all their men and can definitely rate them.

WOMEN OVER 30 ARE BETTER BECAUSE...

They know their exact alcohol tolerances.

WOMEN OVER **30** ARE BETTER BECAUSE...

Their nightmares about exams are starting to fade.

WOMEN OVER **30** ARE BETTER BECAUSE...

They don't run out of toilet paper.

WOMEN OVER **30** ARE BETTER BECAUSE...

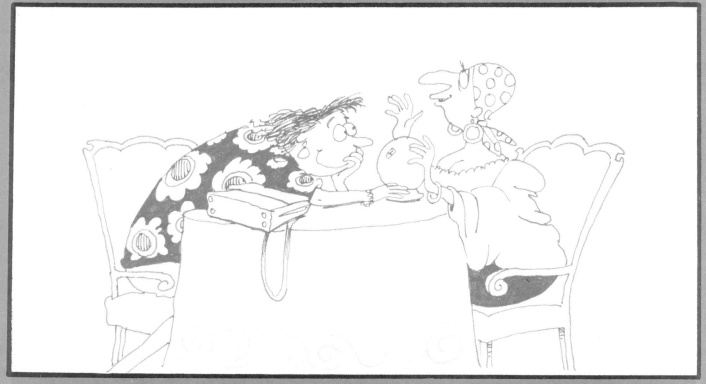

They're almost totally positive that horoscopes are totally bunk.

They've finally learned to ski, golf, run, or whatever rather competently.

They know the proper pronunciation
of at least three white wines and don't let anyone
bamboozle them about which goes well with what.

WOMEN OVER **30** ARE BETTER BECAUSE...

They appreciate the comfort of a few sets of sensible underwear.

WOMEN OVER **30** ARE BETTER BECAUSE...

They've learned that the saleswoman says,
"It's perfect for you" to everyone.

They are smart enough to hire someone to do the cleaning.

WOMEN OVER **30** ARE BETTER BECAUSE...

Pompous sales people no longer intimidate them.

WOMEN OVER 30 ARE BETTER BECAUSE...

*They're resigned to the fact
that when they're dating a man over 40,
he's no longer robbing the cradle.*

WOMEN OVER **30** ARE BETTER BECAUSE...

They no longer worry very much about what the neighbors think.

They consider comfort when buying new shoes.

They start to make some real contributions to their field.

They no longer have to lie on their resumes.

WOMEN OVER **30** ARE BETTER BECAUSE...

They realize no one cares what they did in high school.

They realize the long term effects of sun on their skin.

WOMEN OVER **30** ARE BETTER BECAUSE...

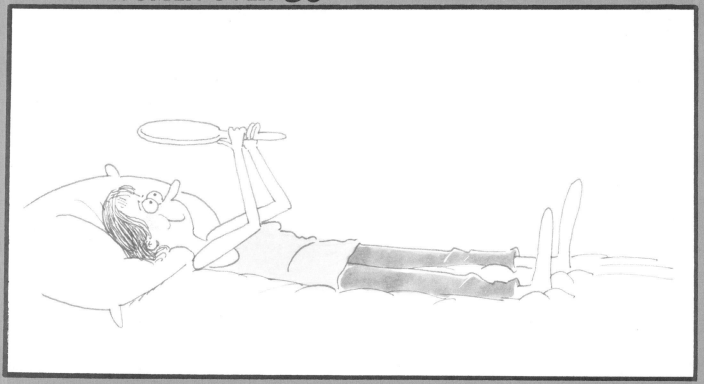

They've given up on self-improvement books, deciding they like themselves just the way they are.

Other books we publish are available at many fine stores. If you can't find them, send directly to us. $7.00 postpaid

2400-How To Have Sex On Your Birthday. Finding a partner, special birthday sex positions and much more.

2402-Confessions From The Bathroom. There are things in this book that happen to all of us that none of us ever talk about, like the Gas Station Dump, the Corn Niblet Dump and more.

2403-The Good Bonking Guide. Great new term for doing "you know what". Bonking in the dark, bonking all night long, improving your bonking, and everything else you ever wanted to know.

2407-40 Happens. When being out of prune juice ruins your whole day and you realize anyone with the energy to do it on a weeknight must be a sex maniac.

2408-30 Happens. When you take out a lifetime membership at your health club, and you still wonder when the baby fat will finally disappear.

2409-50 Happens. When you remember when "made in Japan" meant something that didn't work, and you can't remember what you went to the top of the stairs for.

2411-The Geriatric Sex Guide. It's not his mind that needs expanding; and you're in the mood now, but by the time you're naked, you won't be!

2412-Golf Shots. What excuses to use to play through first, ways to distract your opponent, and when and where a true golfer is willing to play.

2416-The Absolutely Worst Fart Book. The First Date Fart, The Lovers' Fart, The Doctor's Exam Room Fart and more.

2417-Women Over 30 Are Better Because... Their nightmares about exams are starting to fade and their handbags can sustain life for about a week with no outside support whatsoever.

2418-9 Months In The Sac. Pregnancy through the eyes of the baby, such as: why do pregnant women have to go to the bathroom as soon as they get to the store, and why does baby start doing aerobics when it's time to sleep?

2419-Cucumbers Are Better Than Men Because... Cucumbers are always ready when you are and cucumbers will never hear "yes, yes" when you're saying "NO, NO."

2421-Honeymoon Guide. The Advantages Of Undressing With The Light On (it's easier to undo a bra) to What Men Want Most (being able to sleep right afterwards and not talk about love).

2422-Eat Yourself Healthy. Calories only add up if the food is consumed at a table and green M&M's are full of the same vitamins found in broccoli.

2423-Is There Sex After 40? She liked you better when the bulge above your waist was in your trousers. He thinks wife-swapping means getting someone else to cook for you.

2424-Is There Sex After 50? Going to bed early means a chance to catch up on your reading and you miss making love quietly so as not to wake the kids.

2425-Women Over 40 Are Better Because... No matter how many sit-ups they do, they can't recapture their 17-year-old body—but they can find something attractive in any 21-year-old guy.

2426-Women Over 50 Are Better Because... They will be amused if you take them parking, and they know that being alone is better than being with someone they don't like.

2427-You Know You're Over The Hill When... All your stories have bored most acquaintances several times over. You're resigned to being overweight after trying every diet that has come along in the last 15 years.

2428-Beer Is Better Than Women Because (Part II)... A beer doesn't get upset if you call it by the wrong name; and after several beers, you can go to sleep without having to talk about love.

2429-Married To A Computer. You fondle it daily, you keep in touch when you're travelling and you stare at it a lot without understanding it.

2430-Is There Sex After 30? He thinks foreplay means parading around nude in front of the mirror, holding his stomach in; and she found that the quickest way to get rid of a date is to start talking about commitment.

2431-Happy Birthday You Old Fart! You spend less and less time between visits to a toilet, your back goes out more than you do and you leave programming the VCR to people under 25.

2432-Big Weenies. Why some people have big weenies while other people have teenie weenies; as well as the kinds of men who possess a member, a rod and a wang—and more!

2433-Games You Can Play With Your Pussy. Why everyone should have a pussy; how to give a pussy a bath (grease the sides of the tub so it can't claw its way out); and more!

2434-Sex And Marriage. What wives want out of marriage–romance, respect and a Bloomingdale's chargecard; what husbands want out of marriage –to be allowed to sleep after sex.

2435-Baby's First Year. How much will it cost, secrets of midnight feedings, do diapers really cause leprosy and other vital info for parents.

2436-How To Love A New Yorker. You love a New Yorker by pretending to understand their accent, sharing a parking space and realizing they look at "Out of Towners" as new income.

2437-The Retirement Book. Updates the retiree on Early Bird Specials, finding their bifocals and remembering things like paying for the book.

2438-Dog Farts. They do it under the table, in front of the TV, and after devouring some animal they caught in the yard. This book describes them all.

2439-Handling His Midlife Crisis. By treating him like a child when he wants to feel young again and consoling him when he goes from bikinis to boxer shorts.

2440-How To Love A Texan. You love a Texan by agreeing that their chili is just a mite hot, humoring them when they refer to their half acre as a ranch and rushing to help when their belt buckle sets off a security alarm.

2441-Bedtime Stories for your Kitty. Kitties love a story before bedtime and this book guarantees to keep their attention; Goldisocks and the 3 Teddy Bears, The 3 Little Kittens, and more.

2442-Bedtime Stories for your Doggie. This book of tales will keep big doggies as well as puppies entranced every night with stories like The 3 Billy Dogs Gruff, The Little Doggie That Could and many more.

2443-60 With Sizzle! When your kids start to look middle-aged and when your hearing is perfect if everyone would just stop mumbling.

Ivory Tower Publishing Co., Inc., 125 Walnut St., P.O. Box 9132, Watertown, MA 02272-9132   Tel: (617) 923-1111